BEFORE THE DINOSAURS
Coloring Book

JAN SOVAK

DOVER PUBLICATIONS, INC.
Mineola, New York

INTRODUCTION

Before the Age of Dinosaurs (the Jurassic period of the Mesozoic era in the Earth's past), a great diversity of reptiles evolved in a variety of climates and environments. Many of these creatures lived on land, while the habitat of others was freshwater or the oceans. During the course of millions of years, some of these reptiles developed many of the characteristics of modern mammals.

Fossil records of the skeletal structures of these animals show that in many cases the same kinds of creatures lived on what now are widely separated continents. This evidence of the geographic distribution of these animals supports the theory that, prior to the Jurassic period, a single landmass (named Pangaea by scientists) existed on Earth. During the Jurassic period, the northern and southern parts of this great landmass began to separate into two smaller masses, which have been named Laurasia and Gondwanaland. Still later, during the Cretaceous period, these two landmasses began to break up into the continents we know today, which gradually moved to the positions they now occupy. After the continents separated, distinct lines of animal evolution developed within each, so that never again were the same species native to South Africa and Antarctica, or to India and Brazil.

In *Before the Dinosaurs Coloring Book,* artist Jan Sovak has illustrated some of the little-known, vast array of variations within the class Reptilia that existed prior to the evolution of the dinosaurs. Included are a few creatures that appeared during the Devonian and Carboniferous periods of the Paleozoic era; many that flourished during the Permian period at the close of that era; and others that thrived later, during the Triassic period of the Mesozoic. The period covered is from about 350 million years ago to about 200 million years ago. The animals are shown foraging for food, fighting with predators or prey, swimming, running, and even gliding through the air. Few of these creatures survived into the Jurassic period, when dinosaurs were the dominant form of life on Earth. However, the descendants of some of the mammal-like reptiles—the mammals—went on to become the most successful form of animal life.

Bibliographical Note

Before the Dinosaurs Coloring Book is a new work, first published by Dover Publications, Inc., in 1999.

International Standard Book Number
ISBN-13: 978-0-486-40568-1
ISBN-10: 0-486-40568-0

Manufactured in the United States by Courier Corporation
40568005
www.doverpublications.com

Stethacanthus was an early form of shark that lived from the Late Devonian to the Late Carboniferous period. It was more than 2 feet long. Its most notable features were an anvil-shaped dorsal fin topped with sharp toothlike projections, and another such bristling patch on the top of its head. The function of these clusters is a matter of speculation.

An early amphibian, *Crassigyrinus* had a fishlike body with a long tail and tiny limbs, which may indicate that it had returned to a completely underwater life. It had large eyes, which enabled it to hunt in dark waters, and its long jaws were studded with sharp teeth.

A plant-eating reptile, *Edaphosaurus* had a very small head, with many small, sharp teeth of a single kind. It had vertical spines of bone supporting a panel of skin above its back, resembling that of carnivorous *Dimetrodon*, which hunted *Edaphosaurus*. The panel *Edaphosaurus* carried was distinguished by small horizontal projections of bone at intervals on the vertical spines.

Eryops, a powerful, 5-foot-long carnivorous amphibian, lived during the Early Permian period in what is now Texas. An active predator, it ate fish as well as smaller amphibians.

Dimetrodon, a pelycosaur that reached 10 to 11 feet in length, lived during the Early and Middle Permian period, in what is now Texas. A sharp-toothed predator, it absorbed and released heat through a segmented panel of skin stretched over bones that rose from its vertebrae. A network of blood vessels in this panel raised the cold-blooded animal's body temperature relatively quickly in the morning sun, enabling this hunter to pursue its prey. Without such a mechanism, the animal's body temperature would have remained low after a cold night in the desert climate.

Diadectes, which was either an advanced amphibian or an early reptile, was about 5 to 6 feet long. It had broad, blunt teeth, suitable for grinding up plant fiber.

Casea, a plant eater about 4 feet long, was small in comparison to many of its pelycosaur relatives. Its head was small and its broad body housed a large digestive organ within the wide rib cage. *Casea* had no teeth in the lower jaw, but had thick, blunt ones in the upper jaw, and small teeth set into the palate, for grinding tough plants such as ferns.

Cacops was an amphibian well adapted to life on land. About 16 inches long, it had long jaws in a large head (a third of its total body length), bony plates armoring its backbone, and thick legs. A membrane that stretched across a broad opening behind each eye served as an eardrum.

Diplocaulus, which lived in North America during the Late Pennsylvanian and Early Permian periods, was among the lepospondyl amphibians, all of which were extinct by the end of the Permian period. Its body and skull both were flat. The head was a curved triangle of bone, with a point on either side. The eyes and nostrils were on the upper surface of the skull, but the small mouth was below. Two pairs of tiny legs hung from the elongated body. *Diplocaulus* probably never emerged from the water. It breathed through gills behind the head, often spent long periods immobile in one underwater spot, and fed on small fish on the bottom.

A slender, 16-inch-long reptile, *Mesosaurus* is known to have lived in South America and southern Africa during the Early Permian period. Its long tail and broad hind feet aided this lake-dweller in swimming. The creature's long jaw held many needle-like teeth. Those in the creature's lower jaw fit into gaps between those in the upper jaw.

10

Trimerorhachis, about 2 feet long, lived in what is now Texas during the Permian period. It was among the amphibians that were named labyrinthodonts ("maze teeth"), because the enamel of their teeth was folded in such a way that a thin slice of tooth appeared to have a maze-like structure.

11

Ophiacodon, a sturdy pelycosaur that lived during the Permian period in what now is Texas, typically was 10 to 11 feet long. It spent much time in lakes and rivers. Its diet consisted mainly of fish.

Sphenacodon, with a typical length of 10 feet, was among the sphenacodont pelycosaurs—the first large terrestrial carnivores. Its narrow skull, long jaws, and array of canine, incisor, and cheek teeth were typical of its family. Powerful back muscles helped it to launch itself at its prey.

13

Lizard-like *Araeoscelis*, about two feet in length, had long legs, a long neck, and a small head. Its blunt, conical teeth were adapted for crushing the hard coverings of the beetles and other insects it ate.

14

Titanophoneus, a small, herbivorous dicynodont, lived during the Early Permian period in North America. Like other dicynodonts—some of which were smaller and some of which were much larger—it was notable for two large, curving tusks set in the upper jaw, but had few other teeth. In place of a full set of teeth, it used powerful jaws like a turtle's beak, operated by strong muscles, to cut through tough plant material.

Venyukovia was a large herbivore with many small teeth and a few large teeth in front. It lived in northern Asia during the Middle Permian period.

Lycosuchus was a six-foot-long carnivore that lived during the Middle Permian period. Like other therocephalians, it had a large hole in its skull behind each eye.

Estemmenosuchus had a massive shield of bone at the top of its skull, and a variety of protrusions from its head. A nasal "horn" like that of the modern rhinoceros was accompanied by large bony projections from each cheek, and a pair of branched horns above its eyes. In addition, a raised crater atop its head contained a pineal "eye"—a light-sensitive organ.

Elginia, a pareiasaur that lived in what is now Scotland, during the Late Permian period, was about 10 inches long. A hornlike projection angled upward from the upper back portion of its skull.

Helicoprion was a primitive shark-like fish that lived in fresh water, throughout the Northern Hemisphere and in Australia, during the Permian period. Both its upper and its lower jaw supported a spiral tooth whorl, somewhat like the serrated blade of a circular saw. Its dorsal fin extended the entire length of its body, from a point behind the head.

Kingoria, a medium-size dicynodont, lived during the Late Permian period. A mammal-like reptile with a diet of plants, it was hunted by carnivores.

Moschops, a heavy-skulled, broad-bodied dinocephalian, lived in South Africa during the Late Permian period. The thickness of the bones in its forehead suggests that these animals butted heads in fights for dominance within the herd, as do modern goats and bighorn sheep.

Relatively long hind legs were set directly under its body, but its broad forelegs turned out to the sides. The chisel-like teeth in its short jaws were used for biting off plant material.

Titanosuchus, an 8-foot-long carnivore, lived in what is now South Africa during the Late Permian period. It was among the dinocephalians, characterized by their massive skulls. Its huge canine teeth and its sharp incisors were used to kill and eat large plant-eating dinocephalians.

Peltobatrachus, a slow-moving amphibian more than 2 feet long, lived in Africa, in what is now Tanzania, in the Late Permian period. Its body was covered by tough bands of protective plating, like those of modern armadillos.

Youngina was a small (18 inches long), slender, lizard-like reptile with a long tail and a tapering skull. It lived in what now is South Africa, during the Late Permian period.

Scutosaurus, an advanced pareiasaur, stood on legs set directly beneath its body and thus able to support its great weight. Like other pareiasaurs, it was a herbivore with a massive body, small hornlike protuberances on its head, and bony plates extending from the skull. Pareiasaurs spread from southern Africa to Europe and Asia during the Permian period, but became extinct by its end.

Lycaenops, a 2-foot-long predator that lived in South Africa during the Late Permian period, preyed on plant-eating, mammal-like reptiles such as the numerous dicynodonts. In this scene it has just killed a 1-foot-long lizardlike reptile, *Galechirus,* which may have been an early variety of dicynodont. *Lycaenops* had long canine teeth in both the upper and lower jaws; its other teeth were smaller. Some species among both the herbivorous prey and the carnivorous hunters had developed mammal-like characteristics of skeleton, skull, teeth, and stance.

Weigeltisaurus lived in what now are England and Germany during the Late Permian period. It could climb a tree with its long ribs folded back, then launch itself and glide as far as 200 feet to another tree, or to the ground, using its large wings of skin stretched over the extended ribs.

Phthinosuchus, an early therapsid about 5 feet long, lived in what is now Europe, during the the Late Permian period. It is thought to be an evolutionary link between the pelycosaurs and the therapsids, which were advanced reptiles and the direct ancestors of modern mammals.

Protorosaurus lived in the deserts of what now is Europe, during the Late Permian period. A lizardlike reptile, it had long legs that enabled it to catch insect prey, and a neck supported by seven elongated vertebrae. It is the earliest known of the archosaurs—the "ruling reptiles," a subclass of Reptilia that were ancestors of the two orders of dinosaurs, as well as other, nondinosaur orders of animals.

Procynosuchus was an early cynodont that lived during the Late Permian period in what is now South Africa. This 2-foot-long creature was adapted for aquatic life. Its limbs were paddle-like; the rear of its body and its tail were flexible, enabling a side-to-side swimming motion; and its tail was flattened, which provided more surface area to make it an efficient aid in swimming.

Sauroctonus was a "saber-toothed" reptile—so called because of its large upper canine teeth. Classified as a gorgonopsian theriodont, it lived in what is now Europe, during the Late Permian period. These predators could run after their prey, because they had evolved legs that were set directly under their bodies, with all the major leg bones moving in the vertical plane, rather than the horizontal.

Bauria had teeth and a skull like those of mammals, but a reptilian lower jaw and remnants of a bar of bone behind the eyes that was typical of reptiles. It seems to have had space in its cheeks, next to its back teeth, for storing partially chewed food. Its length is thought to have been somewhat greater than 3 feet.

Lystrosaurus, a dicynodont with a bulky body and a short, vertically oriented face, was geographically widespread during the Early Triassic period. Its feet were formed mainly of cartilage, and it is thought that the animal spent much more time in rivers and lakes than walking on land.

34

The mammal-like reptile *Cynognathus,* which was about the size of a large dog, had a massive head, which featured sharp teeth and strong jaw muscles. A powerful, agile predator, *Cynognathus* could run quickly because its hind legs were placed directly beneath its body.

Kannemeyeria was a dicynodont known to have lived in South Africa during the Early Triassic period. It was about 6 feet long and had a massive head and body. A horny beak protruded above the lower jaw.

Longisquama, a six-inch-long, lizard-like thecodontian, had overlapping scales on most of its body. A row of tall, V-form scales, much taller than the creature's body, rose from its back. What function these unusual structures had is unknown.

Erythrosuchus, with a typical length of nearly 15 feet, was the largest animal known to have existed on land in Early Triassic times. This reptile, which was among the earliest archosaurs, was not numerous in its South African habitat. Its skull was more than 3 feet long. The creature's pointed teeth, which curved backward slightly, were set in sockets.

Thrinaxodon was a small cynodont that thrived during the Triassic period, in what are now South Africa and Antarctica. A carnivore, it was about 20 inches long and could run quickly on strong legs set directly under its body. Its skeleton shows that it had evolved several characteristics of mammals that were not present in its reptilian ancestors, and it was the first vertebrate that is known to have a distinct chest (with a rib cage protecting the heart and lungs) and lower back. It may have been warm-blooded (capable of internally controlling its body temperature) and females may have suckled their young with milk.

During the Triassic period, *Nothosaurus* was plentiful in shallow coastal waters of seas in various parts of the world, but these long-jawed, long-necked creatures did not survive into the Jurassic period. Slender and lizard-like, with relatively long legs and paddle-like feet, these

reptiles reached 10 feet in length (less than some of their nothosaur relatives). Their long, sharp-pointed teeth were efficient for catching fish. *Nothosaurus* could walk on land, and fossil evidence indicates that its young were born in caves and on beaches.

Scaphonyx was a heavy-bodied (about 200 pounds) rhynchocephalian ("beak-head") that is known to have lived in what is now Brazil, during the Middle Triassic period. A down-curved beak protruded from its upper jaw. The beak, together with tooth plates in the mouth (the creature had no regular teeth) probably was used to chop and crush hard-husked fruits.

Oligokyphus was a cynodont that lived beyond the Triassic period, into the Early Jurassic. A small animal, about 18 inches long, it had unusual teeth for a cynodont. There were no canine teeth—a large gap existed where they would have been in the row of teeth. The front teeth were incisors, and behind the gap were cheek teeth with many cusps, like the teeth of modern animals that eat seeds and nuts.

Tanystropheus, a 20-foot-long creature closely related to the lizards, had a small head at the end of a long, stiff neck supported by eleven elongated vertebrae. The tubular neck was three-quarters of the animal's entire length, and may have been used to enable seizing fish and mollusks while standing on the seashore. This reptile lived in Europe, in and near the sea, during the Middle Triassic period.

Massetognathus, which lived in what is now Argentina, during the Middle Triassic period, was a plant eater, unlike the majority of cynodonts. The crowns of its cheek teeth had a pattern of crests and valleys, and the lower teeth fitted into the upper ones. A gap between the cheek teeth and the small canines in the front of the jaw enabled these creatures to pull in their cheeks, as modern rodents do, to keep food in the back of the mouth while it was being chewed.

INDEX